A-Minute-A-Day
High Frequency Words

2019 UK Edition

GW00503303

40 Photocopiable One Minute Challenges
to Improve Reading Skills.

A Teacher Timesaver

by Sheila Crompton

dP

DEBRICH PUBLISHING

2019
PUBLISHED BY
DEBRICH PUBLISHING,
LOCHSIDE FARM, SANQUHAR, DUMFRIESSHIRE. DG4 6EW.

2nd Edition © DEBRICH PUBLISHING 2019

A catalogue record of this book has been lodged and is available from the British Library.

ISBN 978-0-9536023-8-4

WHAT IS A MINUTE A DAY?

A-MINUTE-A-DAY is a series of 3 books, which aim to improve basic reading and mental maths skills, in a challenging yet fun way.

Each book contains a number of photocopiable games, each focusing upon specific groups of letters, words or numbers.

The aim of each game is for the student to give 30 correct *verbal* responses within 1 minute.

No writing skills are required.

Each page or worksheet can be used repeatedly by the student for practice both in school and at home, and progress assessed by the teacher in just A-MINUTE-A-DAY.

WHY A-MINUTE-A-DAY?

A-MINUTE-A-DAY has at its roots a method known as **precision teaching,** which since its inception in 1964 has been adopted by an ever increasing number of teachers. Its proven success in both mainstream and special needs education is indisputable.

The value of precision teaching lies in identifying a specific area of need for a particular child, followed by a daily period of teaching, testing and evaluating progress.

Normally, this process can take around 10-15 minutes of completely undivided attention for a particular child. Whilst this can be considered a short enough period to offer any child, for a teacher without ancillary support and with multiple children requiring similar help, it can often be impossible to achieve.

A-MINUTE-A-DAY offers a new methodology, which enables teachers to offer their students tailored systematic practice and monitoring of progress on a daily basis, whilst drastically reducing the amount of teacher involvement

A-MINUTE-A-DAY HIGH FREQUENCY WORDS

Research has shown that the 25 most common words make up about one third of all printed material, and that a group of 100 words comprises approximately 50% of all words likely to be encountered*.

These are known as *high frequency words.* Mastery will provide a firm foundation upon which reading competence may be achieved. For a child to become a fluent reader, it is recommended that the mastery of a further 120 words is achieved.

A-MINUTE-A-DAY HIGH FREQUENCY WORDS supports this approach to reading, and in addition to focusing upon the first 220 essential words, further widens the pupil's sight vocabulary by including groups of words based around specific themes.

* Source: The Reading Teacher's Book of Lists, Fourth Edition, © 2000 by Prentice Hall Authors: Fry, Kress & Fountoukidis

KEY FEATURES OF A-MINUTE-A-DAY

ENCOURAGES PARENTAL INVOLVEMENT

So many teachers battle stoically on, alone, and yet there is a vast and frequently untapped source of support in the form of parents and family who are invariably eager and capable of participating in their child's education.

FUN - YET CHALLENGING. EVERY CHILD CAN ENJOY SUCCESS.

Parents want their children to learn, so let us show them how they can help, but LET IT BE FUN, not with tedious lists, but with games. Above all, let us ensure that homework at Primary level is a shared experience for parent and child.

SAVES HOURS OF HOMEWORK PREPARATION AND MARKING

Often, there is insufficient time to set homework on a regular basis for primary children, and still less time to check it.

If therefore, there is some way in which teachers could direct parents to an area of need for their child, which they would practise for no more than 10 minutes a night, all that is required of the teacher, is A-MINUTE-A-DAY to monitor the child's progress.

IMPROVEMENT IS MEASURABLE AND EASILY UNDERSTOOD BY THE CHILD

Children love competition - provided that the pressure is not too great. Let them compete against themselves. If they can answer six questions one night, make sure they can answer eight the next, and so on. It does not matter where you begin, it's how much you improve that counts. Often the slowest children are able to enjoy the most success, because they have the room for the greatest improvement.

SPEED PLUS ACCURACY EQUALS FLUENCY.

Each game requires the child to give 30 correct *verbal responses* within 1 minute.

This gives adequate opportunity for accurate responses. There is little value in encouraging speed at the expense of accuracy. As the child becomes more skilful, and the first goal is achieved, the time limit may be reduced. For most of the games, a time limit of thirty seconds should not be beyond the ability of the average child.

BLANK GAMES TO SUPPORT FURTHER READING WORK.

Included at the end of the book are three content free games, which may be used for further phonic work or for sight vocabulary. When used for the latter i.e. when phonically unrelated words are to be learnt, it may be wise to limit the number of new words to suit the ability of the individual child, and to use the remaining spaces to repeat and therefore reinforce those words which offer most difficulty.

Sheila Crompton 2019

A-MINUTE-A-DAY HIGH FREQUENCY WORDS

CONTENTS

RECEPTION

1. EGGS	2. BUBBLES	3. SHELLS	4. LITTLE DOG	5. RAINDROPS
I	are	big	it	he
go	the	she	at	am
come	of	and	play	all
went	we	they	no	is
up	this	my	yes	cat
you	dog	see	for	get
day	me	on	a	said
was	like	away	dad	to
look	going	mum	can	in

YEARS 1 - 2

6. SAVE	7. BALLOON RACE	8. DUCK RACE	9. LUCKY DIP	10. JAM TARTS
about	may	with	home	too
can't	people	an	must	pocket
her	there	do	put	back
many	will	his	time	ball
over	again	much	your	door
then	did	pull	as	how
who	him	three	dig	new
after	more	would	house	saw
could	push	another	name	took
here	these	don't	ran	rabbit

YEARS 1 - 2

11. BUTTERFLY	12. HOT X BUNS	13. PUDDLES	14. GARDEN PATH	15. PARTY TIME
down	seen	bed	making	brother
if	two	girl	got	had
next	lived	last	boy	live [d]
school	because	now	little	once
tree	from	say[s]	old	way
carrot	just	been	off	but
be	not	very	so	half
first	should	good	want	love
jump	us	laugh	some	one
night	called	having	water	take

YEAR 3+

16. EGG HUNT	17. STARLIGHT	18. SNOW STORM	19. ORANGES...	20. BUILD A WALL
by	make	ask [ed]	goes	leaves [ing]
has	our	began	gone	show
made	their	being	heard	started
or	when	brought	I'm	stopped
that	came	change	jumped	think
what	help	coming	knew	thought
call [ed]	man	didn't	know	told
have	out	does	leave	tries
than	them	don't	might	turn [ed]
were	where	found	opened	used

CONTENTS Continued

Eggs

Susie lives on a farm.
She is collecting the eggs for her Mum.
Can you help her?

You have one minute to put as many eggs into the basket as you can.

Start here

come · was · look · day · you · went · up · was · come · day · look · you · go · I · went · I · was · up · day · up · look · go · you · was · go · day · I · look · come · I · went · you · go · day

Well Done!

Practise every day.
Do not miss out any words.
Write your score on the back.

1

Bubbles

Sam likes to blow bubbles.

His dog Jack likes to jump up and pop the bubbles!

How many bubbles can you read before Jack pops them?

Start

dog · are · this · going · me · like · of · are · this · we · the · going · going · me · the · like · dog · are · we · this · of · the · going · me · this · we · dog · me · going! · like · are · of · the

POP!

You have just one minute to try.
Practise every day. Do not miss out any words.
Write your score on the back.

Shells

Ken and Jill are hunting for shells.
Can you help them?

You may pick up a shell if you can read the word.
Hurry – in just one minute, the tide will come in!

Start

big   on   they   mum   she   see

mum   she   and   my   big   away

and   they   she   on   away   my

away   see   they   mum   she   on

they   away   big   my   and   see

Practise every day.
Do not miss out any words.
Write your score on the back.

3

A-Minute-A-Day - Debrich Publishing - Copyright 2019

Little Dog

"Oh where, oh where has my little dog gone?
Oh where, oh where can he be?
With his ears so short and his tail so long,
Oh where, oh where is he?"

Can you follow the paw prints to find the dog? You will need to hurry, in case he runs away! You have just one minute to try.

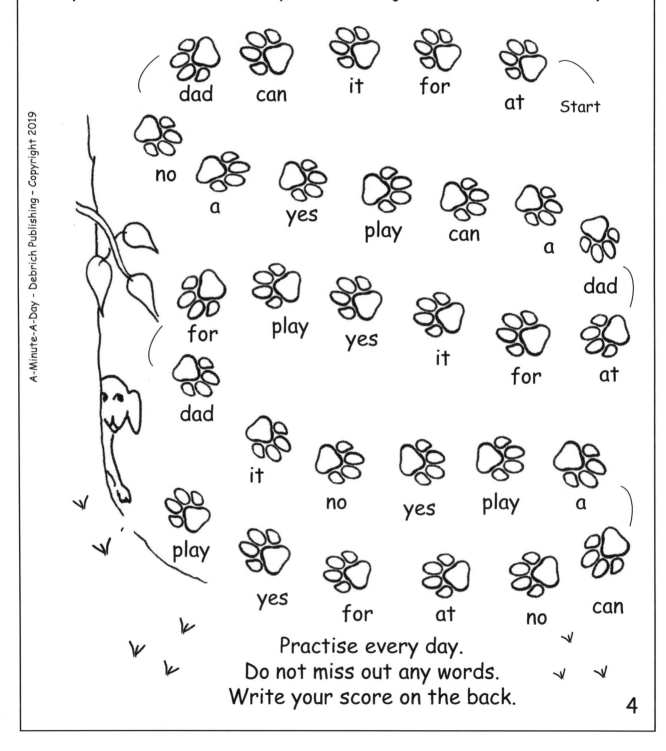

dad can it for at Start

no a yes play can a dad

for play yes it for at

dad

it no yes play a

play yes for at no can

Practise every day.
Do not miss out any words.
Write your score on the back.

4

Raindrops

"Rain rain go away,
Come again another day."

It's starting to rain!
The bus arrives in one minute but if you hurry,
you'll have time to run home for your umbrella!

Start

he · am · said · all · is · cat · said · am · all · get · get · he · is · to · in · in · cat · to · all · said · get · all · said · cat · am · in · is · he · get · to

A-Minute-A-Day – Debrich Publishing – Copyright 2019

Practise every day. Do not miss out any words.
Write your score on the back.

5

Save!

Joe plays football for the school team.
He is a brilliant goalie!

You have just one minute
to see how many goals you can get past him.

Practise every day.
Do not miss out any words.
Write your score on the back.

6

Balloon Race

The race has just started.
Can you read all the words
before the balloons drift away?
You have one minute to try.

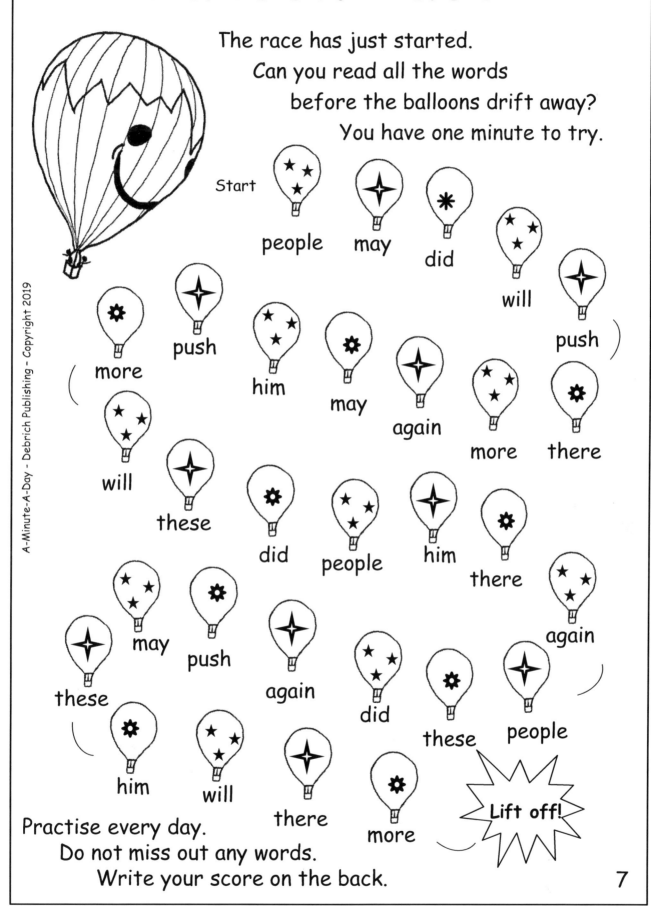

Start

people   may   did   will   push

more   push   him   may   again   more   there

will   these   did   people   him   there   again

these   may   push   again   did   these   people

him   will   there   more   **Lift off!**

Practise every day.
Do not miss out any words.
Write your score on the back.

A-Minute-A-Day - Debrich Publishing - Copyright 2019

Duck Race

The ducks are racing down the river.
Can you read all their names
before they reach the winning post?
You have one minute to try.

Start

three

an

his

do

don't

another

his

with

would

pull

three

much

don't

do

with

another

pull

an

much

an

with

do

would

three

pull

his

another

would

much

don't

Practise every day.
Do not miss out any words.
Write your score on the back.

Well done!

8

☆ Lucky Dip ☆

It is the school Summer Fayre.
The children will win a prize if they can read
the name on the parcel.
Can you help them?
You have one minute to read them all.

Start

Practise every day.
Do not miss out any words.
Write your score on the back.

9

Jam Tarts

The Queen of Hearts
She made some tarts,
All on a summer's day.
The Knave of Hearts
He stole those tarts,
And took them clean away.

Can you chase the Knave and get the Queen's tarts back?
Hurry, he is a fast runner and will be gone in 1 minute!

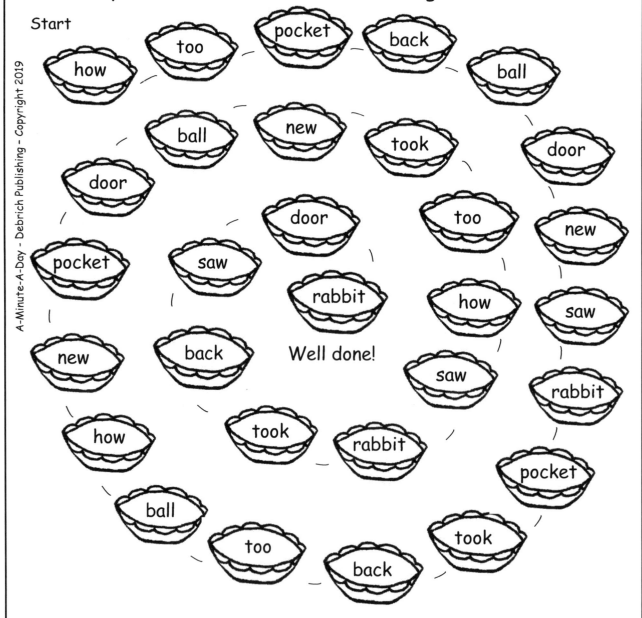

Start

how · too · pocket · back · ball · ball · new · took · door · door · too · new · pocket · saw · door · how · saw · rabbit · new · back · Well done! · saw · rabbit · how · took · rabbit · pocket · ball · too · back · took

Practise every day. Do not miss out any words.
Write your score on the back.

10

Butterfly

The butterfly is sipping nectar from each flower but she may only visit a flower if she can read the word.
Can you help her?
You have one minute to read as many words as you can.

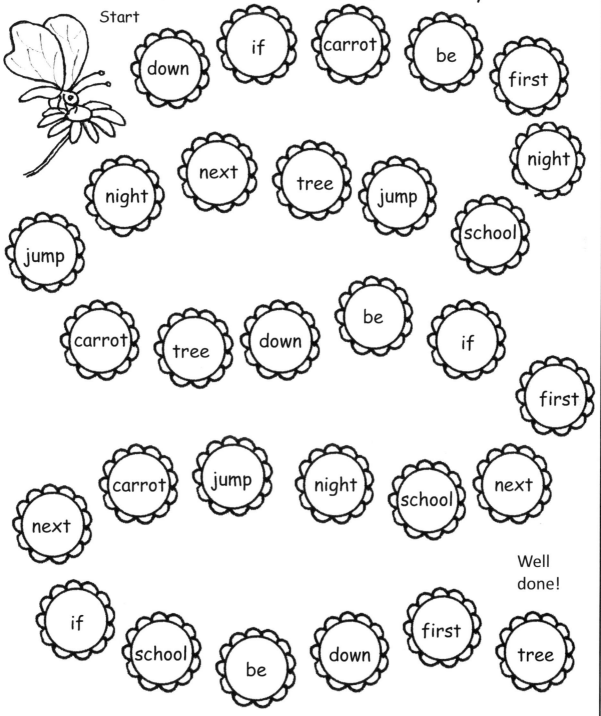

Start

down · if · carrot · be · first · night · next · tree · jump · school · night · jump · carrot · tree · down · be · if · first · next · carrot · jump · night · school · next · if · school · be · down · first · tree

Well done!

Practise every day. Do not miss out any words.
Write your score on the back.

Hot Cross Buns

Hot cross buns!
Hot cross buns!
One a penny, two a penny,
Hot cross buns!

Can you help the baker to sell all his hot X buns?
You may only sell a bun if you can read the word.

You have just one minute to try!

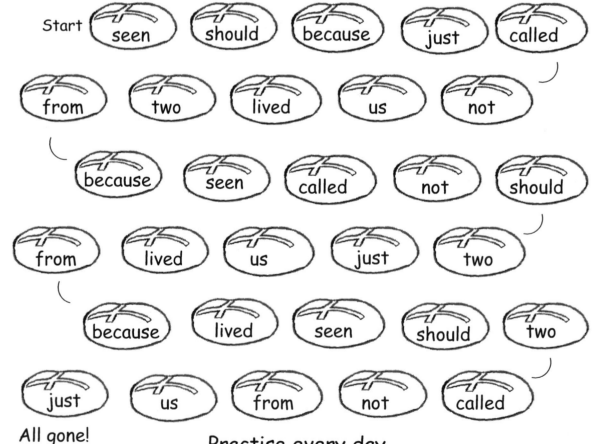

Start   seen   should   because   just   called

from   two   lived   us   not

because   seen   called   not   should

from   lived   us   just   two

because   lived   seen   should   two

just   us   from   not   called

All gone!

Practise every day.
Do not miss out any words.
Write your score on the back.

Puddles

Doctor Foster went to Gloucester,
In a shower of rain.
He stepped in a puddle,
Right up to his middle,
And never went there again!

Take care that you don't fall into these puddles!
See how quickly you can read all the words.
You have just 1 minute to read them all!

Start

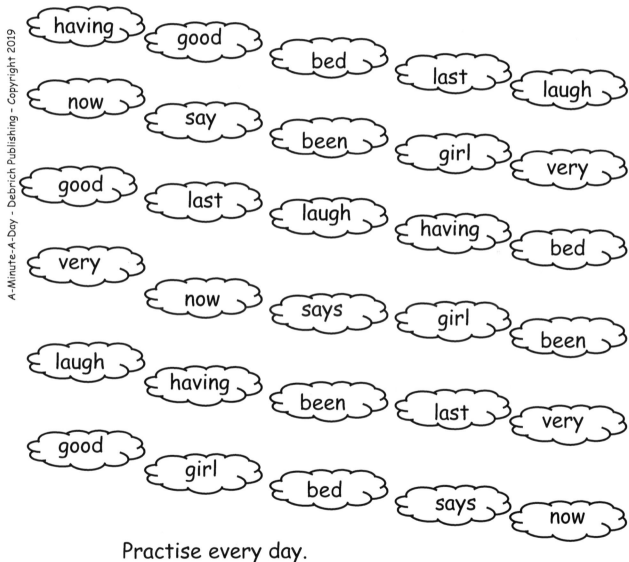

Practise every day.
Do not miss out any words.
Write your score on the back.

13

Garden Path

Tom's dad has laid a stepping stone path in his garden.
See if you can you read the word on every stone.
You may colour a stone when you can read the word.

You have one minute to try!

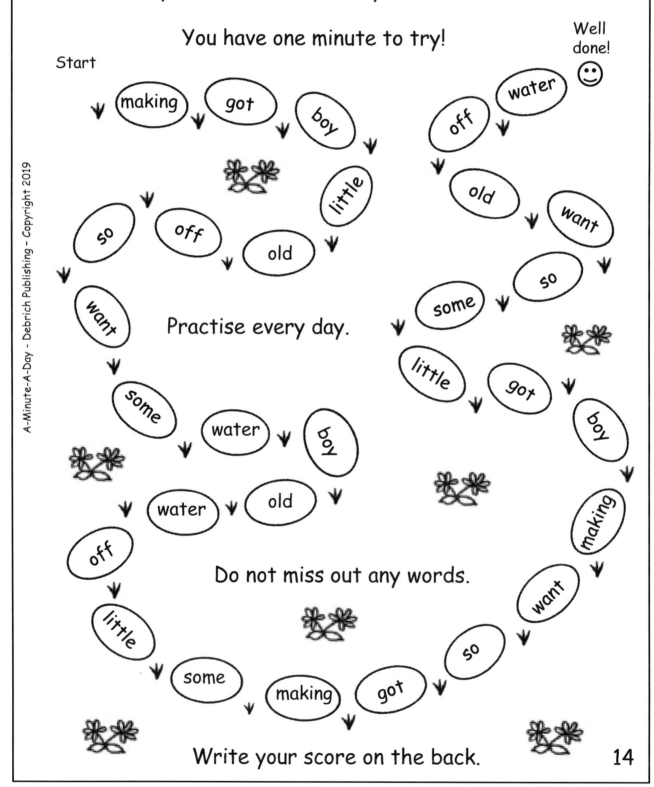

Start

Well done!

Practise every day.

Do not miss out any words.

Write your score on the back.

14

Party Time

Jan's Mum has made buns for the party.
Can you read the words on every bun,
before they are put into the box.
You have one minute to try!

Start

brother	had	lived	once	way
but	half	love	one	take
live	way	brother	but	had
half	take	love	once	one
once	lived	love	had	way
half	but	one	brother	take

Practise every day.
Do not miss any words.
Write your score on the back.

15

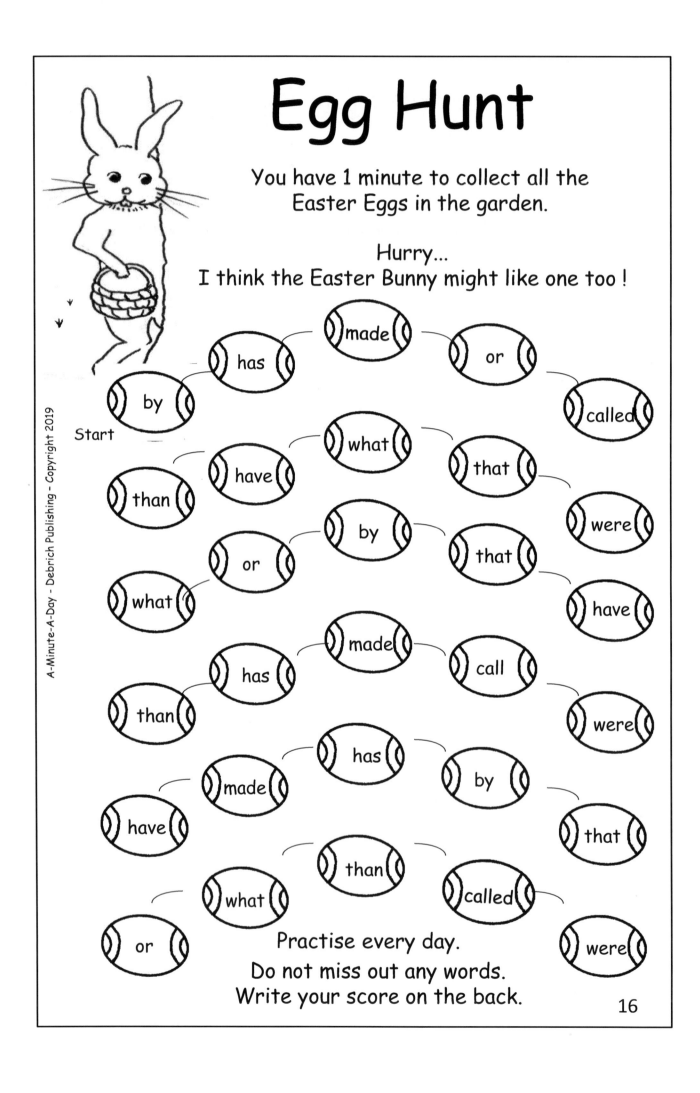

Egg Hunt

You have 1 minute to collect all the
Easter Eggs in the garden.

Hurry...
I think the Easter Bunny might like one too !

Start

Practise every day.
Do not miss out any words.
Write your score on the back.

16

Starlight...

Star light, star bright,
The first star I see tonight;
I wish I may, I wish I might,
Have the wish I wish tonight.

Start

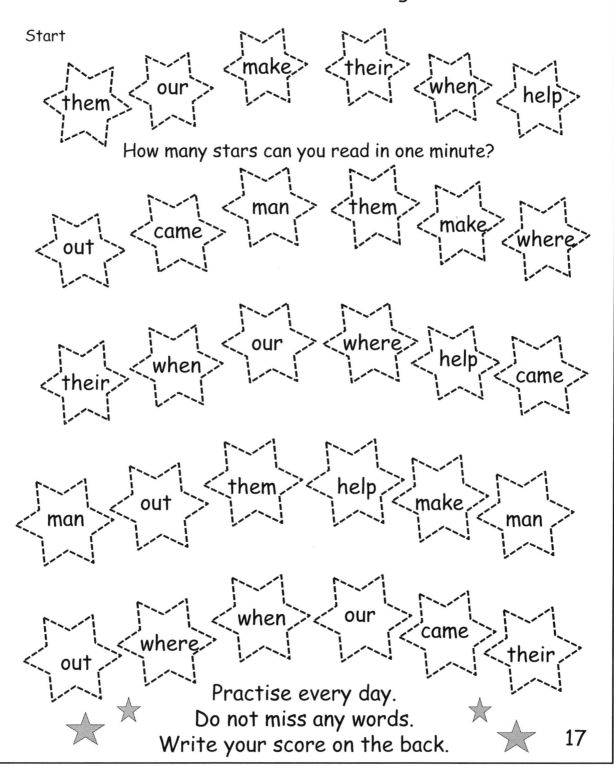

them | our | make | their | when | help

How many stars can you read in one minute?

out | came | man | them | make | where

their | when | our | where | help | came

man | out | them | help | make | man

out | where | when | our | came | their

Practise every day.
Do not miss any words.
Write your score on the back.

Snow Storm

It is a windy day.
The snowflakes are falling fast.
Can you read their names
before they are covered by more snow?

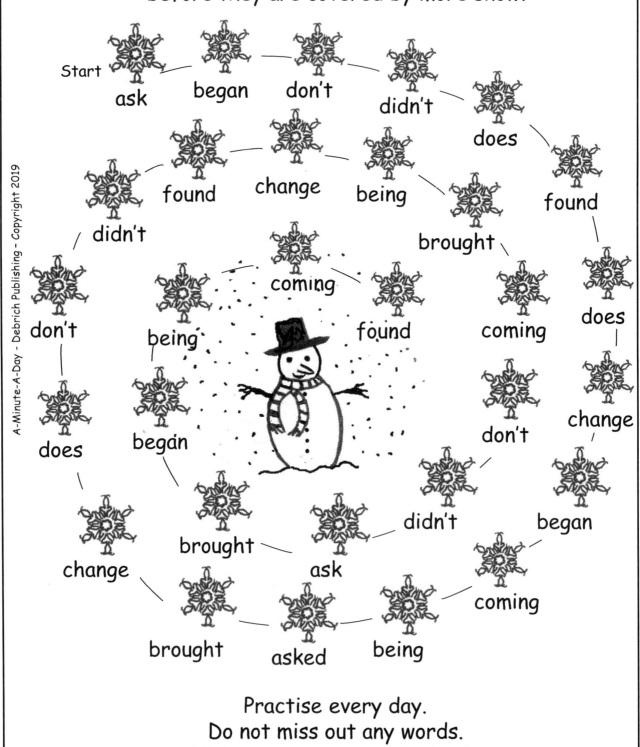

Start
ask   began   don't   didn't   does   found
found   change   being   brought   does
didn't   coming   found   coming   change
don't   being   don't   began
does   begán   brought   ask   didn't   began   coming
change   brought   asked   being

Practise every day.
Do not miss out any words.
Write your score on the back.

18

Oranges and Lemons

♪♪ Say the bells of St Clement's ♪♪
You owe me five farthings say the bells of St Martin's

Can you read all the words belonging to these oranges and lemons?
You have just one minute to read as many as you can!

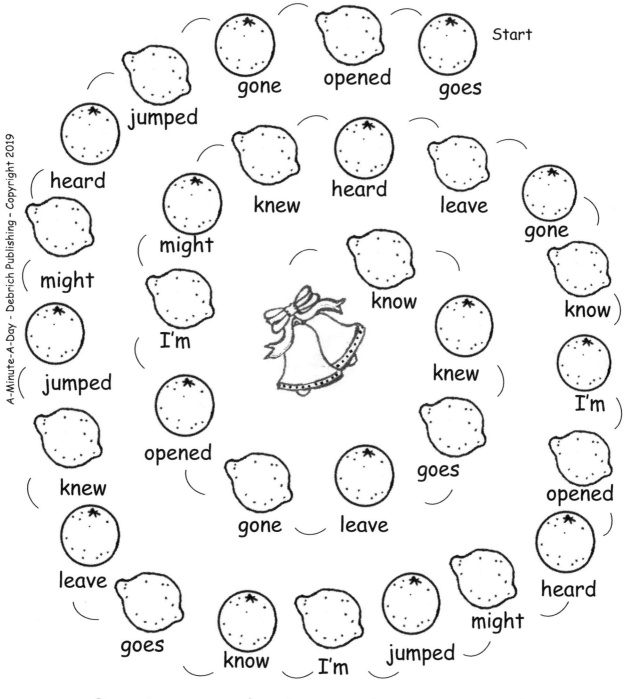

Practise every day. Do not miss out any words.
Write your score on the back.

19

Build a Wall

Uncle Bill needs lots of bricks to build a wall in his garden.
Can you help him to collect the bricks?

You may only pick up a brick if you can read the word on it.

Start

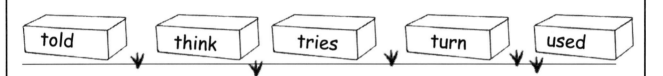

leaves started stopped show thought

told think tries turn used

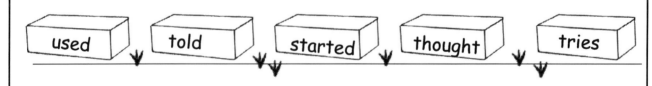

show turn leaving stopped think

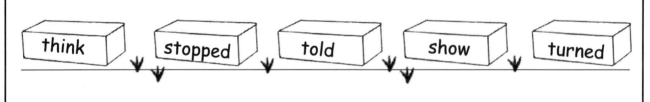

used told started thought tries

think stopped told show turned

tries started leaves used thought

Practise every day.
Do not miss out any words.
Write your score on the back.

20

Agility Class

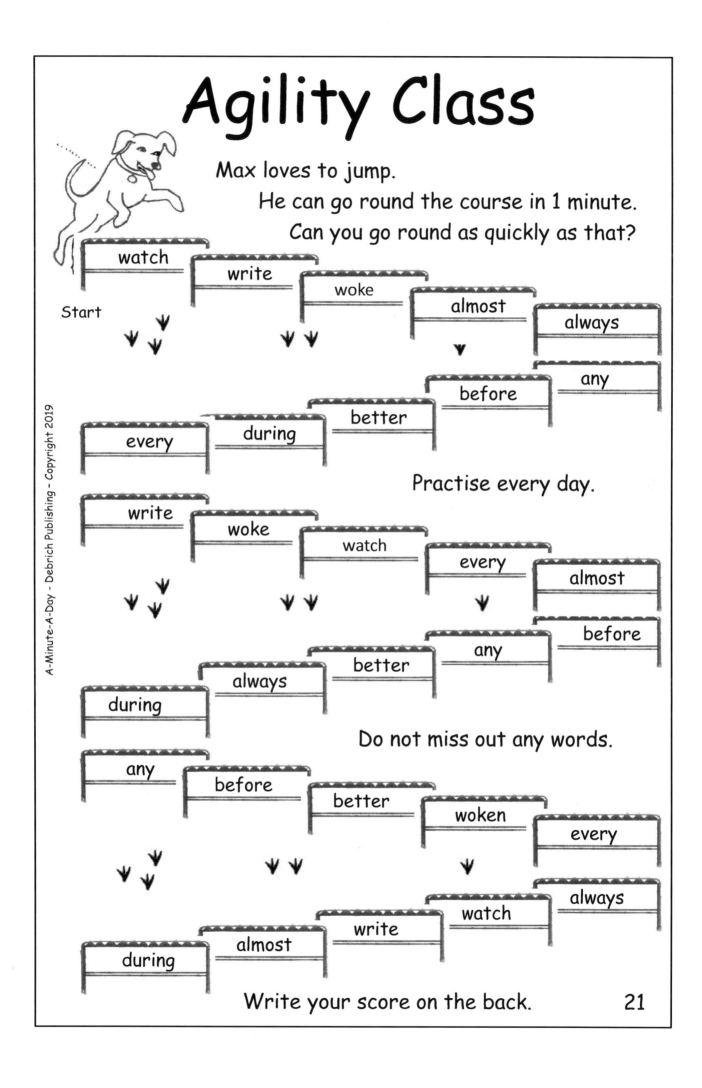

Max loves to jump.

He can go round the course in 1 minute.

Can you go round as quickly as that?

watch

write

woke

almost

always

any

before

better

Start

every

during

Practise every day.

write

woke

watch

every

almost

before

any

better

always

during

Do not miss out any words.

any

before

better

woken

every

always

watch

write

almost

during

Write your score on the back.

A-Minute-A-Day - Debrich Publishing - Copyright 2019

Flash Cards

The children are trying to read all the words before they go out to play.
Can you help them?

HURRY, the bell will ring in just one minute!

Start

never	number	often	only	second
sometimes	first	half	morning	much
only	sometimes	second	often	number
never	much	morning	half	first
number	never	often	much	only
morning	second	sometimes	half	first

Practise every day.

Write your score on the back.

22

Feathers

The robin is collecting feathers
to line her nest.
Can you help her?
You have 1 minute to collect as many as you can.

Start

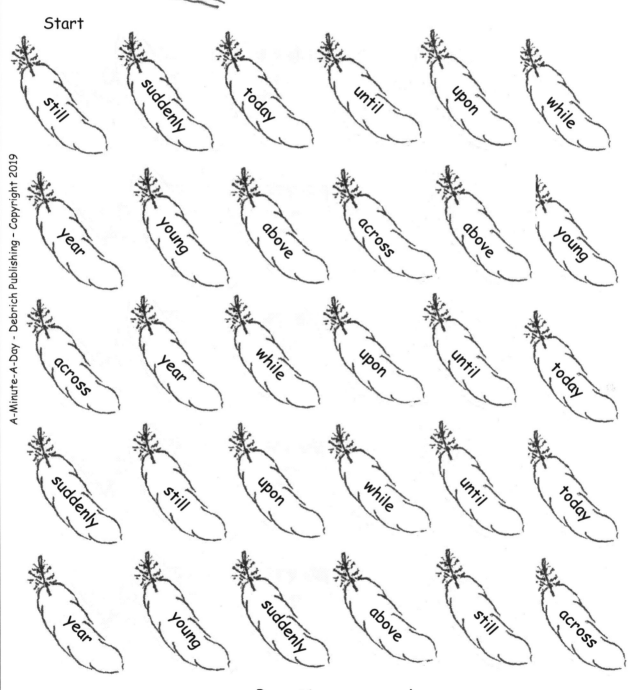

still   suddenly   today   until   upon   while

year   young   above   across   above   young

across   year   while   upon   until   today

suddenly   still   upon   while   until   today

year   young   suddenly   above   still   across

A-Minute-A-Day - Debrich Publishing - Copyright 2019

Practise every day.
Do not miss out any words.
Write your score on the back.

23

Ladybird

The ladybird is hungry.
She is searching the garden for some aphids for dinner.

See if you can help her to find some.

You have just one minute to try!

Start

following

along *

also

between

around

below *

both *
*

different

inside

both *
*

between

different

high *

around

high

* also
*

around

along *

following

inside
*

high

* below
*

between

also *
*

along

inside

both *

Practise every day.
Do not miss out any words.
Write your score on the back.

24

Books

John is searching for a special book.
Can you help him by reading each title?

You have just 1 minute to try.

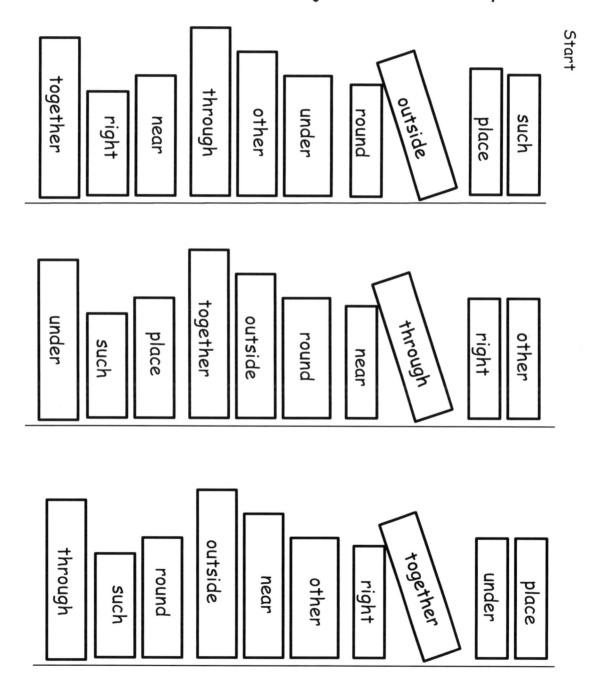

together | right | near | through | other | under | round | outside | place | such

under | such | place | together | outside | round | near | through | right | other

through | such | round | outside | near | other | right | together | under | place

Practise every day. Do not miss out any words.
Write your score on the back.

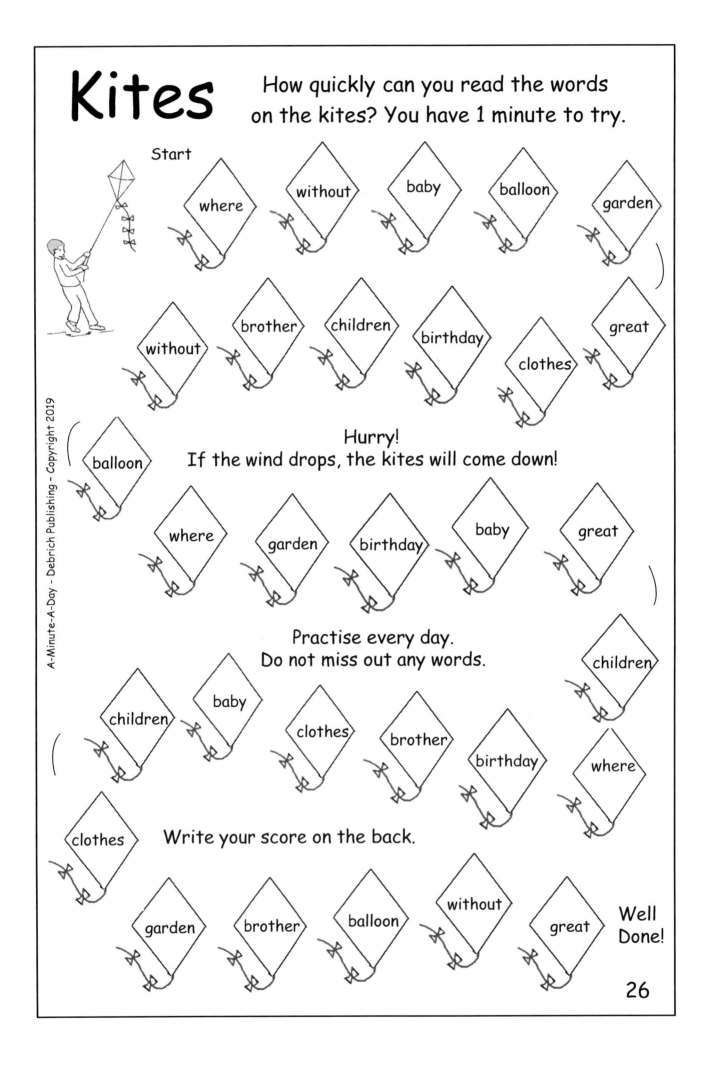

Kites

How quickly can you read the words on the kites? You have 1 minute to try.

Start

where · without · baby · balloon · garden

without · brother · children · birthday · clothes · great

Hurry!
If the wind drops, the kites will come down!

balloon

where · garden · birthday · baby · great

Practise every day.
Do not miss out any words.

children · baby · clothes · brother · children · birthday · where

clothes · Write your score on the back.

garden · brother · balloon · without · great · Well Done!

A-Minute-A-Day - Debrich Publishing - Copyright 2019

Swallows

The weather is getting cold.
Soon the swallows will fly away to a warm country for the winter.
Can you read the name on each bird before it leaves?

Start

head
happy
something
heard
sure

worked
hear
word
those
swimming

heard
swimming
those
happy
hearing

head
heard
work
sure
something

those
word
working
word
sure

happy
swimming
hear
head
something

Practise every day.
Do not miss out any words.
Write your score on the back.

27

Mountain Bike Race

Start

Are you ready? Draw yourself on the bike … (Psst don't forget your helmet!)

How many obstacles can you clear in one minute?

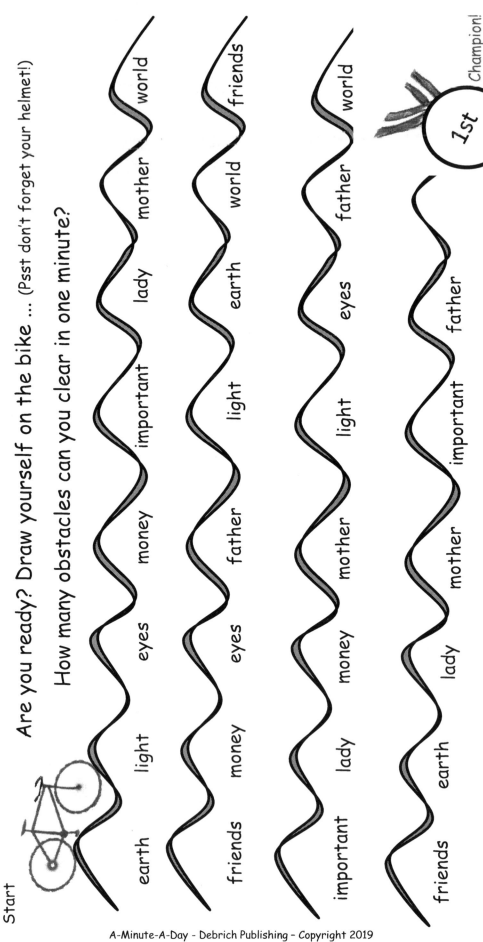

earth · light · eyes · money · important · lady · mother · world

friends · money · eyes · father · light · earth · world · friends

important · lady · mother · money · light · eyes · father · world

friends · earth · lady · mother · important · father

1st

Champion!

Practise every day. Do not miss out any words. Write your score on the back.

28

Scrabble

W H Y

O W N

Start

W H O L E

W I N D O W

S I S T E R

S O U N D

S M A L L

W H I T E

Sue is playing Scrabble.
Can you read all the words
she has made?

S O U N D

P A P E R

W A L K I N G

You have one minute to try.

W H Y

W I N D O W

S M A L L

W H I T E

S I S T E R

W I N D O W

P A P E R

Practise every day.

W H O L E

Do not miss out any words.

O W N

W H I T E

S M A L L

W A L K

S I S T E R

W H O L E

Write your score on the back.

P A P E R

S O U N D

W A L K E D

O W N

W H Y

29

A-Minute-A-Day – Debrich Publishing – Copyright 2019

Days of the Week

Solomon Grundy was born on a Monday,
Christened on Tuesday, Married on Wednesday,
Ill on Thursday, Worse on Friday,
Died on Saturday, Buried on Sunday,
And that was the end of Solomon Grundy!

How quickly can you read the days of the week?
See if you can read them all in one minute.

Start

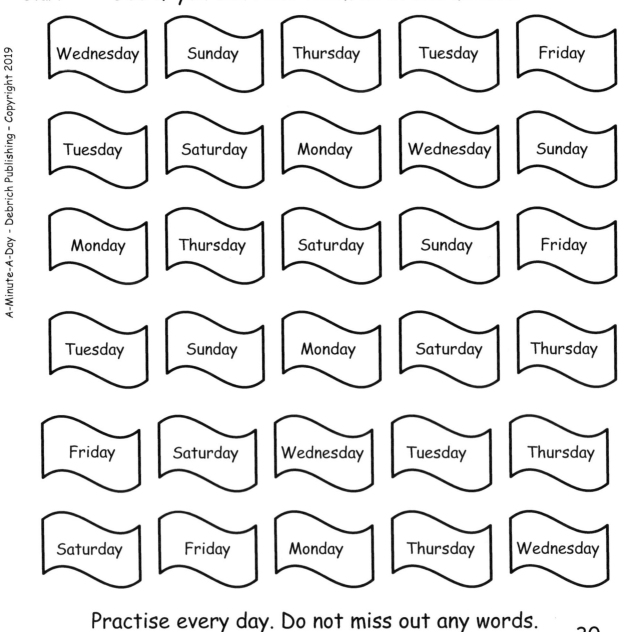

Wednesday	Sunday	Thursday	Tuesday	Friday
Tuesday	Saturday	Monday	Wednesday	Sunday
Monday	Thursday	Saturday	Sunday	Friday
Tuesday	Sunday	Monday	Saturday	Thursday
Friday	Saturday	Wednesday	Tuesday	Thursday
Saturday	Friday	Monday	Thursday	Wednesday

Practise every day. Do not miss out any words.
Write your score on the back.

Months

30 days have September,
April, June and November.
All the rest have 31,
Except for February alone,
which has 28 days clear
and 29 in each leap-year.

Bob has been learning the names
of the 12 months of the year.
He can read them all in 1 minute.
Can you beat him?

Start

June	September	August	February	April

October	January	March	November	May

July	December	June	May	February

August	April	September	January	October

May	February	October	April	July

March	December	August	January	November

Practise every day.
Do not miss out any words.
Write your score on the back.

Numbers 1-10

Do you know this number rhyme?

One, two, three, four, five,
Once I caught a fish alive,
Six, seven, eight, nine, ten,
Then I let it go again

Why did you let it go?
Because it bit my finger so.
Which finger did it bite?
This little finger on the right.

Now see if you can read all these numbers very quickly.
Try to read them all in one minute!

Start

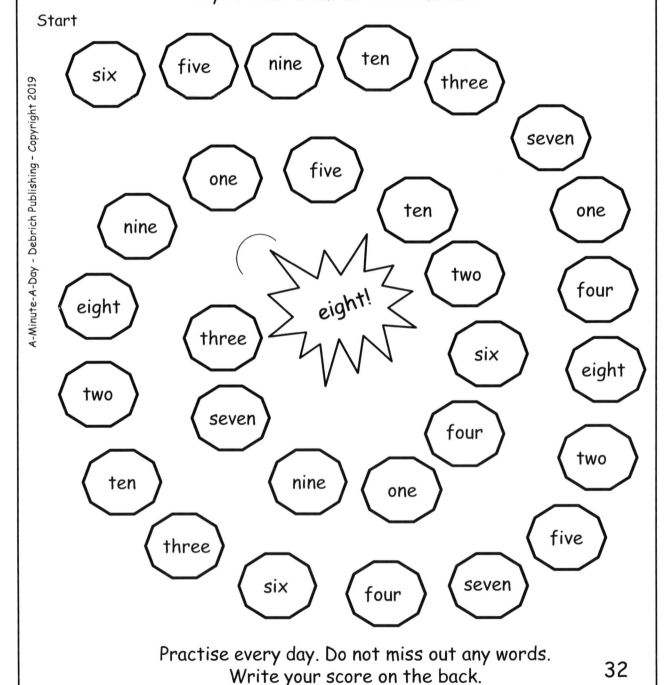

Practise every day. Do not miss out any words.
Write your score on the back.

Numbers 11-20

Whenever Alfie finds it hard to sleep, his Mum says 'Try counting sheep.'

Start

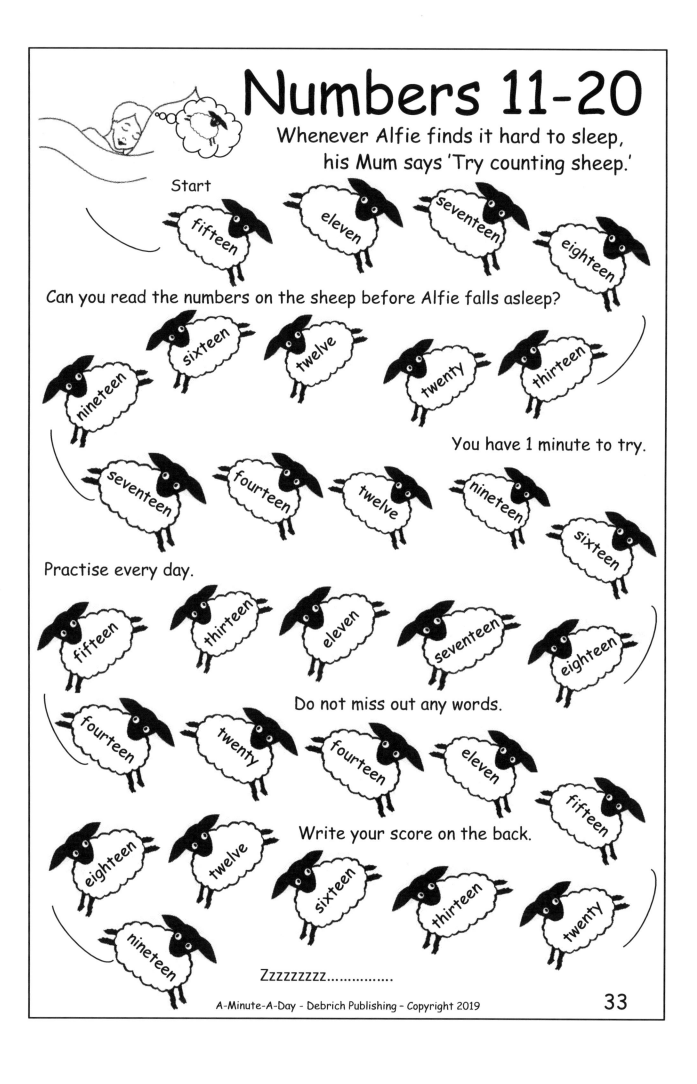

Can you read the numbers on the sheep before Alfie falls asleep?

You have 1 minute to try.

Practise every day.

Do not miss out any words.

Write your score on the back.

Zzzzzzzzz...............

Colours

The children are each allowed to choose a sweet
if they can read the colour on the wrapper.
Can you read the colour of every sweet?

Start

orange   yellow   red   blue   green

You have just one minute to try!

purple   brown   white   black   pink

yellow   purple   pink   blue   brown

Practise every day.

black   orange   green   white   red

orange   blue   purple   brown   yellow

Do not miss out any words.

black   red   pink   white   green

Write your score on the back.

Question Words

The children are visiting the art gallery.
They are asking lots of questions.

What is the name of the picture?

Who painted it?

When was it painted?

What kind of paint was used?

How many of these question words can you read?
See if you can read them all in 1 minute.

Start

who? where? when? which? why? how?

what? when? why? who? which? where?

who? why? how? which? what? when?

which? when? what? who? where? who?

how? why? where? how? what? which?

Practise every day.
Write your score on the back.

Home Address

This is my address

I am going to practise reading every part of my address.
My challenge is to do it all in 1 minute without stopping!

Start

PS Remember to include the postcode!

Practise every day.
Write your score on the back.

36

My School Address

All the parts of the address have been jumbled up.
Can you read them all in 1 minute without stopping?

Start

Practise every day.

Do not miss out any words.

Write your score on the back.

Hoofprints

The gate is open and the horse has escaped!
Follow the hoofprints to find him.
You may colour a hoofprint if you can read the word.
See if you can read them all in one minute.

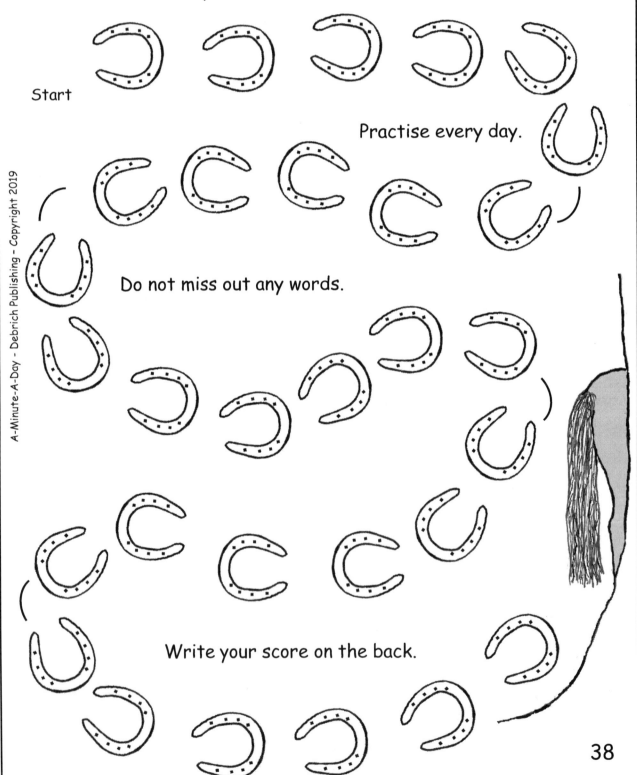

Start

Practise every day.

Do not miss out any words.

Write your score on the back.

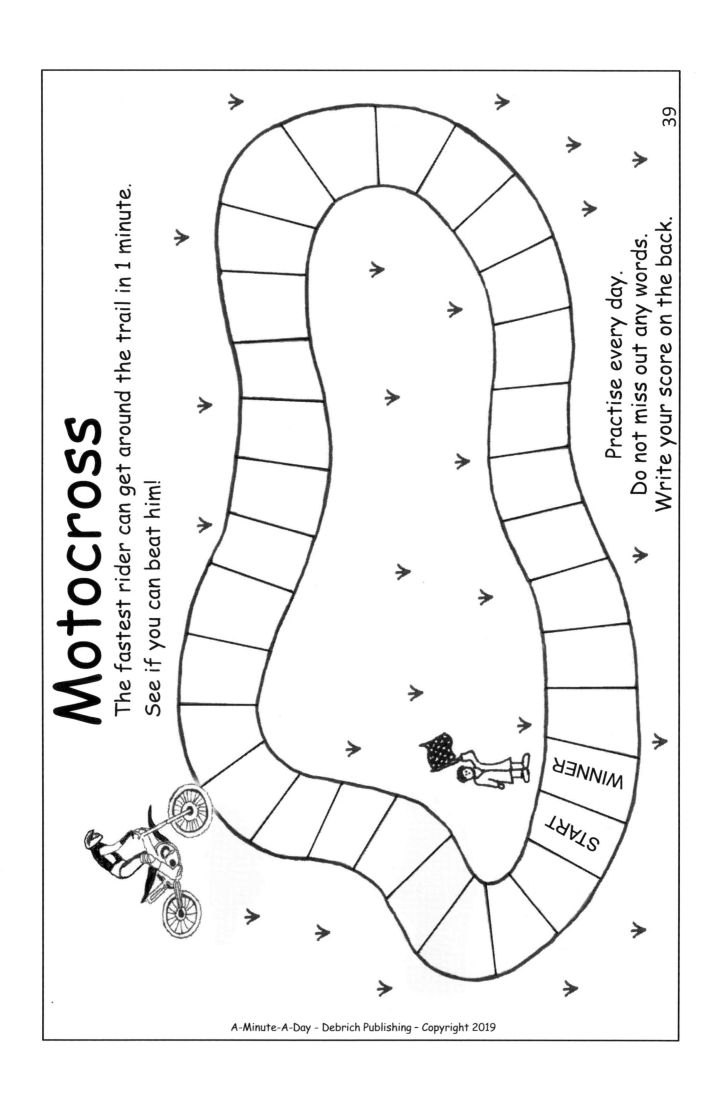

Motocross

The fastest rider can get around the trail in 1 minute.
See if you can beat him!

Practise every day.
Do not miss out any words.
Write your score on the back.

START

WINNER

39

Traffic Jam

A lorry has broken down on the motorway and there is a long traffic jam.
See if you can read the name on every vehicle before the road reopens.

Start

Hooray!

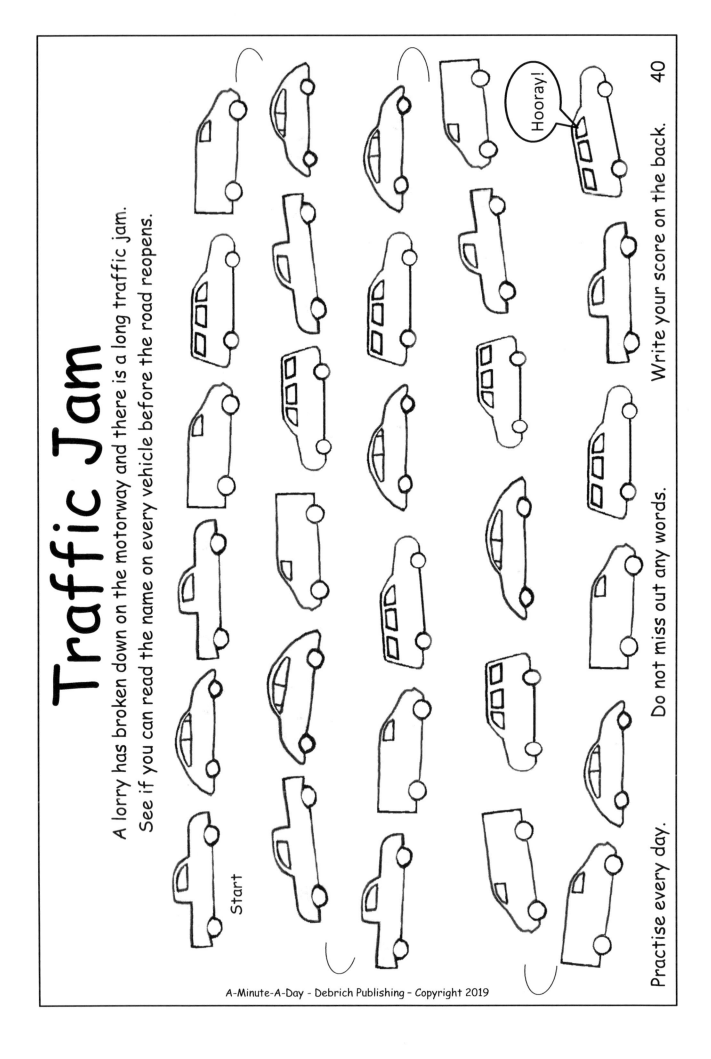

Practise every day.   Do not miss out any words.   Write your score on the back.

A-MINUTE-A-DAY - HIGH FREQUENCY WORDS

RECORD SHEET (1)

	Start Date	Finish Date
RECEPTION		
1. EGGS (I, go, come, went, up, you, day, was, look)		
2. BUBBLES (are, the, of, we, this, dog, me, like, going)		
3. SHELLS (big, she, and, they, my, see, on, away, mum)		
4. LITTLE DOG (it, at, play, no, yes, for, a, dad, can)		
5. RAINDROPS (he, am, all, is, cat, said, to, in)		
YEARS 1-2		
6. SAVE (about, can't, her, many, over, then, who, after, could, here)		
7. BALLOON RACE (may, people, there, will, again, did, him, more, push, these)		
8. DUCK RACE (with, an, do, his, much, pull, three, would, another, don't)		
9. LUCKY DIP (home, must, put, time, your, as, dig, house, name, ran)		
10. JAM TARTS (too, pocket, back, ball, door, how, new, saw, took, rabbit)		
11. BUTTERFLY (down, if, next, school, tree, carrot, be, first, jump, night)		
12. HOT X BUNS (seen, two, lived, because, from, just, not, should, us, called)		
13. PUDDLES (bed, girl, last, now, say[s], been, very, good, laugh, having)		
14. GARDEN PATH (making, got, boy, little, old, off, so, want, some, water)		
15. PARTY TIME (brother, had, live[d], once, way, but, half, love, one, take)		
YEAR 3 AND ABOVE		
16. EGG HUNT (by, has, made, or, that, what, call[ed], have, than, were)		
17. STARLIGHT (make, our, their, when, came, help, man, out, them, where)		
18. SNOW STORM (ask[ed], began, being, brought, change, coming, didn't, does, don't, found)		
19. ORANGES (goes, gone, heard, I'm, jumped, knew, know, leave, might, opened)		

A-MINUTE-A-DAY - HIGH FREQUENCY WORDS

RECORD SHEET (2)

YEAR 3 AND ABOVE

	Start Date	Finish Date
21. AGILITY CLASS (watch, write, woke[n], almost, always, any, before, better, during, every)		
22. FLASH CARDS (first, half, morning, much, never, number, often, only, second, sometimes)		
23. FEATHERS (still, suddenly, today, until, upon, while, year, young, above, across)		
24. LADYBIRD (along, also, around, below, between, both, different, follow[ing], high, inside)		
25. BOOKS (near, other, outside, place, right, round, such, through, together, under)		
26. KITES (where, without, baby, balloon, birthday, brother, children, clothes, garden, great)		
27. SWALLOWS (happy, head, heard, something, sure, swimming, those, word, hear[ing], work [ed] [ing])		
28. BIKE RACE (earth, eyes, father, friends, important, lady, light, money, mother, world)		
29. SCRABBLE (walk [ed] [ing], paper, sister, small, sound, white, whole, why, window, own)		
30. DAYS (Monday, Tuesday, Wednesday, Thursday, Friday, Saturday, Sunday)		
31. MONTHS (January, February, March, April, May, June, July, August, September, October, November, December)		
32. NOS. 1 - 10 (one, two, three, four, five, six, seven, eight, nine, ten)		
33. NOS. 11 - 20 (eleven, twelve, thirteen, fourteen, fifteen, sixteen, seventeen, eighteen, nineteen, twenty)		
34. COLOURS (red, blue, yellow, green, purple, orange, brown, black, white, pink)		
35. QUESTIONS (who, where, when, which, why, how, what)		

CONTENT FREE

	Start Date	Finish Date
36. HOME ADDRESS		
37. SCHOOL ADDRESS		
38. HOOFPRINTS		
39. MOTOCROSS		
40. TRAFFIC JAM		

"A-MINUTE-A-DAY" HIGH FREQUENCY WORDS

Dear _____

I am writing to ask for your help with the work which _____ is bringing home from school today.

It relates directly to the stage (s)he is focusing upon at school.

A *maximum* of 15 minutes each day is all that you will need. About ten minutes to practise and one minute to test, in a room free from distractions eg TV, toys etc.

Do not worry if your child's score is low at the beginning. The emphasis is on *improvement*, i.e. if the score is 6 one night, aim for 8 the next and so on.

Above all, keep the session *brief, light-hearted* and remember to give *lots of praise* for effort.

Would you please write your child's score on the back of the sheet and return it to school every day. Thank you.

Signed ....

"A-MINUTE-A-DAY" HIGH FREQUENCY WORDS

Dear _____

I am writing to ask for your help with the work which _____ is bringing home from school today.

It relates directly to the stage (s)he is focusing upon at school.

A *maximum* of 15 minutes each day is all that you will need. About ten minutes to practise and one minute to test, in a room free from distractions eg TV, toys etc.

Do not worry if your child's score is low at the beginning. The emphasis is on *improvement*, i.e. if the score is 6 one night, aim for 8 the next and so on.

Above all, keep the session *brief, light-hearted* and remember to give *lots of praise* for effort.

Would you please write your child's score on the back of the sheet and return it to school every day. Thank you.

Signed ....

Printed in Great Britain
by Amazon